We Share the Same Darkness

We Share the Same Darkness

Poems by
William F.M. Currie

William Currie
warrior.poet.wfmc@gmail.com

ISBN 9781527259294

Printed in the United States of America

First Printing, 2020

Illustrations by Agnes Zakaria
Editing: Tell Tell Poetry | www.telltellpoetry.com
Design: Cover&Layout | www.coverandlayout.com

This book is dedicated to my daughter, Miya, who inspired me to write this book to show her that, no matter what your dream is, if you want it badly enough, you will do what it takes to make it happen.

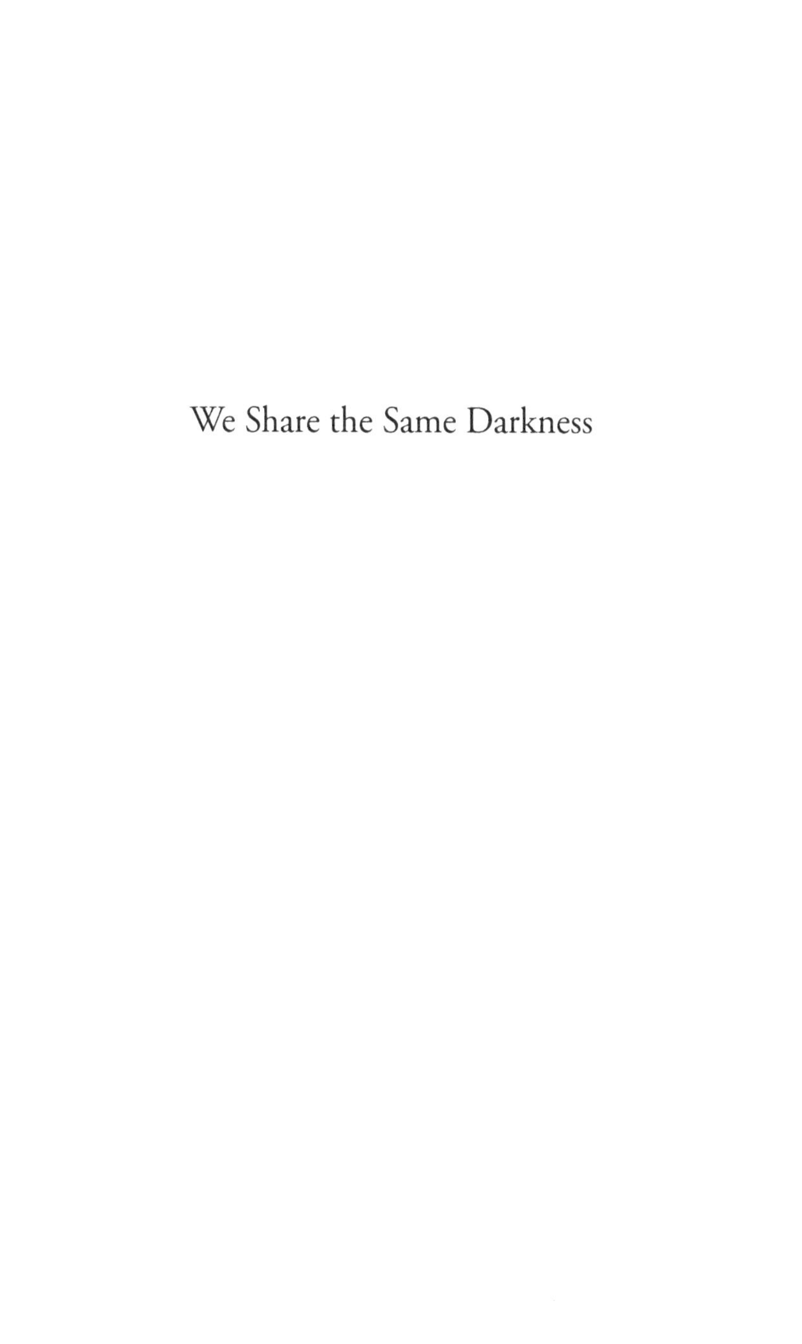

We Share the Same Darkness

Contents

Prologue   1
   Unlocked Potential   2

Suffering in Silence   5
   Past Life   7
   The Machine   9
   Battlefield Prayer   11
   Doon in the Dirt   13
   Lonely Road   15
   His Untold Story   17
   Invisible Wounds   18
   Can You Escape?   21
   As I Sit Here Contemplating Death   23
   Emotionally Mute   25
   Destructive Choices   28
   Room with a View   31
   The Vicious Cycle   33
   Revenge   34
   Panic Attack!   37
   Used Parts of the Machine   39
   Salt Water   43

Hope from the Abyss   45
   Rough around the Edges   49
   The Choice to Change   55
   Strength through Art   59
   Hope from the Abyss   61
   Be Here Now   63

The Invisible Darkness   64
Fear of the Unknown   67
Phoenix   70
Gratitude   73

About the Author   75

Prologue

Unlocked Potential

I woke up this morning and began to rhyme.
I have no idea why as this
was my first time.
A release of emotion,
a big ocean wave,
unlocking a talent—am I being naïve?

How does this happen? Has it always been there?
Am I becoming more self-aware?
An ability unlocked; it was just missing the key.
Was it the loss of a love or just the misery?

In person, my emotions refused to appear.
Not even empathy for the ones I hold dear.
All they got was my anger, anxiety, and constant fear.
Was unable to show love to the one I held near.

Now onto this paper my heart does bleed.
Showing undiscovered emotions is what I need.
These unused emotions can be transformed into a muse.
Every thought that I have, there's a rhyme that is new.
But my memory is terrible . . . so poems I lose.

As I exhume these feelings from deep within me,
I have this thought whilst I'm writing this poetry:
Would my life have been different with these emotions set free,
maybe saving relationships which failed so drastically?

For now, my writing is the only comfort I know.
I only hope this skill will continue to grow.
I may even find empathy and new emotions. Who knows?

Poetry: my fix.
Who would have known?

Suffering in Silence

Past Life

To look at me, you could never tell
that I've been to a place that can only be described as hell.

In another life, a uniform I wore
that took me away to distant shores.

To war I've been, many battles I've seen,
all to protect my country, my queen.

Fighting vicious battles against the natives of the land
under the blazing hot sun, creating blood-soaked sand.

Bullets rained, lives extinguished, graves unknown,
never again would hero soldiers return home.
We were just young men trying to survive.
Only the fortunate of us managed to leave those places alive.

I've earned these medals I pin upon my chest.
Now time is the enemy that will bring about my death.

When I'm laid to rest and the body is rotten,
the memory will fade, my story forgotten.

I hope you pass down tales of the soldiers so proud,
keeping their memories alive as they rest in the ground.

The Machine

When I was a boy, to the military I went.
It's still something that to this day I do not regret.
To protect our country, serve the nation,
off we went to training—well, indoctrination.

Break your spirit, grind you down
till there's no individualism left around.
Those who can't hack it don't last that long,
whilst the military rebuilds us all to sing the same song.

Drilled and drilled until you adhere:
never show emotions, never show fear.
Work as a team, never let them down,
never give up till you're laid in the ground.
No need for emotions: they're left in that place.
Now we wear masks of anger upon our faces.
Unnatural to you, you may ask why:
emotions can be the reason some people die.

We move toward gunfire
when normal people run.
Fearless warriors,
every single one.

Every soldier is family, and defend them we would,
even if that means a box made of wood.

Battlefield Prayer

I never thought I'd live this long,
yet I'm still here soldiering on.
During battle, on more than a few occasions,
I took a knee, asked for divine intervention.
I didn't care who answered; I just needed them to listen,
provide me overwatch, safe passage throughout my missions.
Advancing toward the enemy as wild bullets rained,
just trying to survive each awful campaign.

This far in, I'm unsure if I've sold my soul
or made a black-market deal with my guardian angel.
Now I contemplate whose contracts I've signed in blood.
Was this life really worth it? Did I do enough?
I wonder who'll collect when my time's up.
Whoever I bargained with, I'm sure my destination's hell
as access to heaven means "thou shalt not kill."
I've broken that commandment, as far as I can tell.

Will I be caged in hellfire for the rest of eternity?
Or be trapped, stuck waiting in purgatory
with devils and angels fighting for their right
to the claim on my afterlife?
Whatever the outcome, it's out of my control.
I must answer for my life. I'll stand proud and alone.

Doon in the Dirt

Take heed!
When am cauld, buried, and deid,
dinni weep.
For A was a soldier,
an' A lived b' th' sword.
A knew t' outcum A was heedin toward.
A dinni expect nae medal, nae fancy award.
Aw A ask eh ye, ma brothers, is come fin me in th' reorg.

Wir wull drink n' trade stories uv auld times gan bye.

Fir t' rist av ey'ternity, wull wach th' nu sunrise.

Lonely Road

There are some paths you have to walk alone
to find your strength and grow.

These paths are long, winding, and arduous;
some you may not be able to pass.

At times you may feel you're not progressing
as you retrace old tracks.

You may come to crossroads on this journey.
Choose wisely the one you make your destiny.

Once your expedition has ended and the lessons been learned,

my only hope for you is that growth has been felt.

His Untold Story

You would call him a veteran,
but I'm sure he'd disagree.
His service may be done; he's no longer overseas.
But war for this soldier has not yet ended.
He fights battles you cannot see.

He never realised how much it really costs
to lose friends during combat, mourn the loss.
In his mind, his actions take centre stage.
That image of death, it shall never age.
Horrifying, yet he's unable to turn the page.

When taking the lives of the enemy,
he watched as their lives drained,
no empathy for them or their screams of pain.
As their souls dissipated and the bodies grew cold,
he'd think "It was me or them who'd get to grow old."

Now his body bears the scars invisible to you or me.
Darkness haunts his dreams for what seems an eternity.
It tortures his brittle mind with unspeakable imagery.
Regret over untold acts you may class as bravery
replay over in his head and cause him misery.

His enemy can strike at any moment, bring him to his knees.
This the soldier fights alone, and he fights it silently.
All he wants is this conflict to end, to try and claim some victory.
This war was never written down, never part of history.
The enemy this soldier fights against is PTSD.

Invisible Wounds

For I was a sword
with flawless technique,
a shield that protected
the young and the meek.

My strike was just,
swift, and true
as I kept the tyranny
from reaching you.

To all the enemies
I put in the ground,
I was known as a warrior
who would never back down.

A life full of war
left me with unseeable wounds;
for the eyes of the world,
I wear this hero's costume

As I battle the demon
inside of my head,
when we fight, it fills me
with the utmost dread.

He tears my thoughts
limb by limb.
I feel it's the only conflict
I'll never win.

This crippling enemy
wants to see my demise
as it resides patiently
behind my eyes.

Can You Escape?

I am the darkness, the destroyer of worlds.
You will never escape my strangling hold.
Stories of me, your children are told.
For eternity I'll live, never growing old.

I feed off your fear, regret, guilt, and pain
till I'm the only thought that remains.
Once I'm able to take control of your soul,
then I'll convince you to end it all.

Why do I torment my host, orchestrate their death?
Well, there's a little secret I'll have to confess.
What if I told you that I don't really exist,
that I'm just conjured up by your subconscious?

Your own whispering thoughts trying to defeat you.
If you got some help, you could work it through.
You may even be able to take back control,
escape my darkness, release the hold.

I've given you some pointers, and you may disagree,
but I still think that you'll never defeat me.
I'll see you again on the battlefield soon,
where we'll once again fight under the moon.

As I Sit Here Contemplating Death

I can't get the word out of my head.

Suicide. Suicide. It's infesting my brain.
Could this be the way to end my pain?
These words burrow deep inside,
blackening my thoughts and corrupting my mind.

I stare at my reflection in the mirror.

I'm just not that strong; maybe it's just a matter of time.
Life or death, that choice is mine.
I think about the loved ones that I'd leave behind.
Maybe in time they'd understand, forgive me.
I've tried to hang on, but I can't see clearly.

This time I will follow through, complete the act.

I stand on the chair, look at the wall.
It's the only time I've felt so tall.
Take the rope, tie it 'round my neck
as I wonder about the things left unsaid,
like the reason I think I'm better off dead.
I'll whisper it to the reaper with my last breath.

Emotionally Mute

Emotions.
You think I don't have them, that I harbour only rage,
but I was molded to have an emotional cage.
Emotions are high and deep inside of me,
yet I'm unable to express them properly.

I hold on to the negatives for such a long time;
they start out as seeds, then grow into great vines.
Lack of compassion, no empathy for you,
you felt like I lacked love for you, too.

You tried to get me to express how I feel.
All you got was a stone wall every time you'd appeal.
You gave me every ounce of your heart and soul,
but your impression of me was I never cared at all.

I did love you, but it was expressed in a different way.
You couldn't feel it, and that eventually pushed you away.
With different perceptions of how things should be,
we really never could coexist in that reality.

I locked you out; that's my burden to bear.
I knew if I wanted to keep you, I had to share—
unlock my emotions, feelings, and display to you my soul.
Unfortunately, my fear is the emotion that overrides them all.

Fear What's Inside

There's an evil that lurks deep within your soul.
Attempt, you must, to keep it in that hole.
If you don't, the darkness will devour you whole.

Destructive Choices

When a cup of darkness is what I consume,
untethered chaos in the universe will resume.
I change into my alter ego,
not a lifesaving, people-pleasing superhero.

Dawn the cloak, apply my mask.
Blackout commences, a psychotic trance.
I care for no one that I see,
for I am the main character in this horror movie.

I become the villain, the one driven by your demise.
When I change, I see hatred in your eyes.
When you see the goodness drain from my soul,
the villain is transformed: I'm ready to go.

Make space for him. I'm coming through.
Like a bull seeing red, we're charging at you.
Death.
Destruction.
Chaos is the goal!
We may even attempt to steal your soul.

When, finally, the darkness dissipates,
consciousness is regained.
Fragmented memories, regret, and shame.
Trying to figure out to whom I've caused pain.

You may ask why I let my villain play,
why I allow him to ruin lives in this sordid way.
Like Jekyll and Hyde, Hulk and Banner,
he is able to navigate my life in a distinctive manner.

For the parts of life I'm not strong enough to manage,
I must pay him homage.
Sometimes the balance tips the wrong way.
Destruction is the price I have to pay.

Room with a View

An island I am, and alone I stand.
I've learned how to survive off of this land.
No help needed; I thrive from the conditions.
I've created this world: my own personal prison.

I put up these walls to lock my issues away.
I like quietness so much, I've decided to stay.
With white sand beaches and clear blue sea,
I guess it's really not that bad of a place to be.

I've told you my story, and you've tried to understand.
You've known my pain but not this man.
You have no comprehension of who I am.
I feel you're trying to break down my emotional dam.

Try to get past the walls and join me here.
But this place can only harbour this monster, my dear.
If you glimpse a real part of me, I fear
you'll never be able to hold me near.

I'll only show you the parts I want you to see.
How could you ever love that hidden part of me?
My fear keeps me from letting you onto the island.
Pushing you away, I watch as you crest the horizon.

So I block out the world, hide from my issues.
As all of my relationships, they'll get misused.
I'll just go back to being the old kamikaze pilot.
My life's just simpler being emotionally silent.

The Vicious Cycle

If you don't learn from your mistakes,
you're destined to repeat them for eternity.
Repeat for eternity, you're destined to.
For eternity, you are destined to repeat them.
Repeat them.
Repeat them over
and over
and over.
Insane you'll feel it's making you.
Till it makes you go insane.
The same actions you'll perform.
You'll perform the actions the same.
The same.
The same.
Expecting a different outcome.
No outcome will be different.
But what were you really expecting
when you repeated the same mistakes?
Now you want a different outcome, and life's full of regret.
So break the cycle now and learn from your mistakes,
so you won't repeat them for eternity—for your own sanity's sake.

Revenge

When you're wronged by another in the worst kind of way,
and you know inside they've done it maliciously—
their perception of you is that you're just weak,
and they think that you'll just turn the other cheek—
try to remember, two wrongs don't make a right.

But to use that proverb on such a day
is a difficult task, I would say.
When the monster consumes you,
no clarity you see,
unsure of the future and what it will be.

Replay the past, feed off the rage;
that good side of you has been locked in a cage.
Control is futile, emotions bright red.
Incapable of logic, you feel only dread.

Blinded by emotion all through the day,
by the urge to hurt, to make them pay.
The righteous intentions of revenge
engulf your imagination; you envision their end.

Take a deep breath, calm yourself down,
relax for a while, lift up that angry scowl.
Sit alone for some time
and clear your mind.

Use this moment to contemplate:
Is it worth being consumed by all this hate?
Is revenge worth the price? Who will pay?
These emotions will corrupt your DNA.

Your body, brain, all systems crash.
Emotionally, you will be unable to last
if you even the score
out of hope that your pain will be no more.

That won't be the case, unfortunately.
You'll reminisce on the deed continuously.
Swapping revenge for regret—that is what this will be—
until it's yourself you're unable to see.

Making things equal won't be the end.
Every action has a reaction in the circle of revenge.
Revenge is a game that nobody wins,
and you'll only collect another sin.

I write these words, but judge you I can't.
And believe me, I'm not just here to rant.
I know there are lines that can't be crossed.
Just be aware that you may get lost.

Choose your path wisely is all I will say,
for I know how hard it will be on that day.

Panic Attack!

When it begins,
it comes from deep within.
Thoughts start racing.
Pores start leaking,
rapid breathing.

Your thoughts start to spin.
You feel the world is closing in.
Encapsulating darkness, tunnel vision.
Pulse rate rises.
Distress in your eyes.

Out of control, your heart pounds.
You can hear its distinctive sound.
Rapid bass drum. Damn, it's so loud.
Can't catch your breath, struggle for air.
All bodily systems are now in despair.

If it keeps up, you'll be laid out on the ground.
As you panic more, spiraling out of control,
regulate your breathing. Try to clear your mind.
This terror will pass, no more dreadful ride.
Beware, these attacks can happen at any time
when anxiety, stress, or fear overwhelm your mind.

Used Parts of the Machine

The military made you a part of the machine.
It made you tough; it made you bleed green.
They expect everything from you, no questions asked,
as you fight alongside your brothers in arms.

A life like this grinds your body haggard
till your cogs are worn, broken, or fractured.
Then when you're discarded, as you're no longer needed,
it's left to the veterans to pick up the pieces.

When your service is over,
no uniform you'll wear.
You may have issues that make you despair.
With anger, anxiety, depression, even PTSD,
you'll now need those emotions you discarded so easily.

From the ground up again, you will have to struggle,
trying to figure out all of this civilian muddle.
Learn compassion, empathy, how to communicate,
or you may find yourself on the wrong side of the gate.

Your family needs emotions—more than you possess—
so, if you want to keep them, then you can guess.
What you'll need to do is open up and try to relate.
You never know, it just might not be too late.

Inspiration

I'm still unsure if this a blessing or a curse.
How many poems does my subconscious deem enough?

Salt Water

Take these feelings, my pain,
this confusion away.
Trap it all in a bottle, corking the top,
so all these ruminating thoughts will stop.

Discard the darkness in the sea,
remove it from deep inside of me.
Let the ocean drown all of my sorrow,
so I once again can embrace tomorrow.

Hope from the Abyss

Stay the Course

Stay on your course when navigating rough seas;
those hurricane winds will soon be a breeze.
With compass in hand, don't deviate from your plan.
You'll soon be on the shores of an exotic new land.

Rough around the Edges

My writing isn't polished; I'm not sure what you'd expect
as writing's never been a part of my natural intellect.
The poor construction, spelling, and grammar aren't caused by neglect.
When I'm trying to express a story, I focus too much on its finer aspects
as I try to build an image for you so that my words will connect.

My poems are but a reflection of me, their creator, their architect.
You'd find I'm odd, quirky, and slightly mad if you had to dissect.
None of the boxes are fitting for me. They are all incorrect.
A few steps—well, a long way—off, I am, from being perfect.
In life I do the best that I can whilst dealing with inner conflict.

I'm working on my flaws, and writing's part of this process:
putting my soul on paper, giving strangers private access.
Facing my fear of criticism, I stand here bearing flesh.
This poetry is for my inner self, never intended to impress.
I just know that for all my life, like my poems,
I'll be a work in progress.

Take Back Control

Do not let fear control you!
Fear is a parasite that stops you from
functioning at your best potential.
Stand up tall,
face forward, and walk through it.
Become it, embrace it, feed on it
until the dominance it has over you is depleted.
Only then can you build strength
and resilience against it
to forever break the grip it has on you.

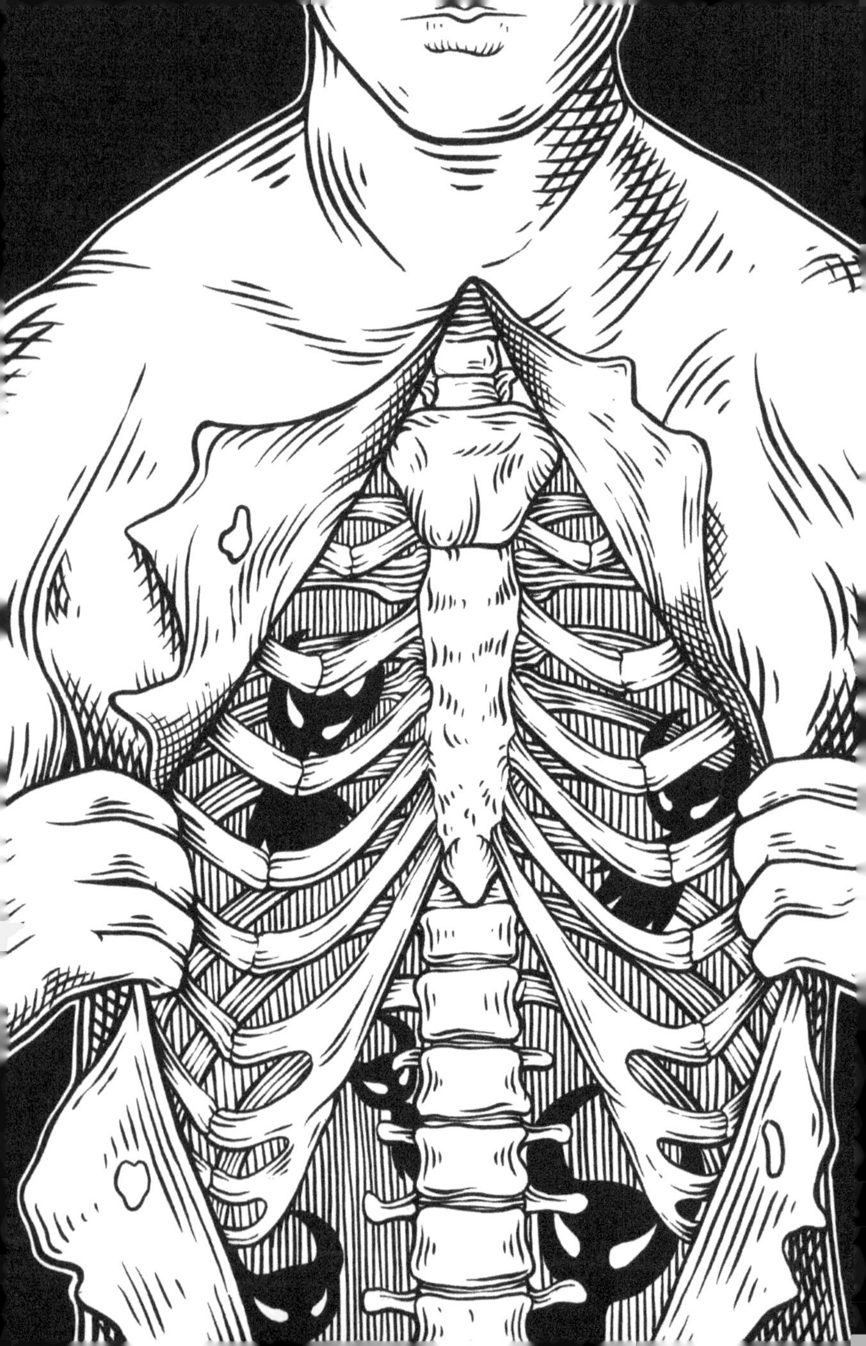

Battle Within

Defeat the things
living under your skin.

The Choice to Change

When you find yourself alone in the darkest of rooms,
where the only light comes from the moon,
where there's an unlocked door you can use if you like,
again, concealing your demons, you can
try to struggle through life.

Or you can stay a while for introspection.
We can work through all those imperfections.
You can cleanse your sins with a confession
and set your life in a new direction.

Then you'll stroll through the door with newfound clarity,
breaking the bonds of your insanity.

Plan B Is Part of the Plan!

Whilst patrolling through some unknown land,
fully equipped with rifle in hand,
be safe, mitigate the risks, devise a plan.
Take every precaution that you can.
Sometimes your path may become traitorous,
so, if you can't be safe, be FUCKING DANGEROUS!

Strength through Art

Showing my poems to work through my fear
of criticism, ridicule, rejection—it's all there.

There's a narrow perception of the poet in people's minds.
They ask why someone would rhyme words on a line.
They think that I'm broken, take pity on me,
unable to comprehend what I can now see.

I've never before expressed emotions this way.
My strengths on the paper in the words I've laid
provide me the power to seize the day.
They can laugh all they want! I don't care what they say.

These words, these emotions, they are all mine;
this passion I found during trying times.
A barrage of words placed upon a page—
some about love, loss, and even rage.

I hope that my words will connect in a way
when someone's needing lifting from a life full of grey;
that briefly, for a second, they'll alleviate someone's pain
and offer a break from reality to step out of their brain.

To those who think poems are just for the weak,
your lives without art must be so bleak.

Hope from the Abyss

Spiraling down into the deep, dark abyss,
one day I found myself up on a cliff.
A choice on that day I had to make,
not entirely sure which would be the mistake.

Would I offer my life for Poseidon to take?
I was just one step down to the crashing sea's wake.
No more confusion, unstable emotions,
I'd end it all. But then I had a new notion.

As I looked to the sky for divine intervention,
I stumbled upon a different perspective:
Maybe this pain was my brain's misconception,
a deep-rooted consciousness deception.

New clarity given to the situation,
I could acknowledge I had an affliction.
I'd share my feelings with people to get it all out.
Damn, if I needed, I'd stand up and shout.

I'm not broken completely, and repairable I am.
As hard as this is to say, I just needed a hand.
Mental health is a killer, so many lives does it take.
If you're feeling this way, like you can't get a break,
please reach out for your own life's sake.

Be Here Now

If you're apprehensive of the future,
panicked on what is yet to be;
intrusive thoughts clouding your mind, causing anxiety;
or you're stuck ruminating on the past, on your indiscretions,
further you'll fall, spiraling into depression.

If your eyes are looking forward or back at the rear,
you'll miss all the magical moments with the ones standing here.
So don't focus on the past or look into the future.
Be here in the now during this adventure.

The Invisible Darkness

When love dissolves to a distant thought,
when their perception of you is riddled with rot,
when they no longer see you or express that they care,
after they strip you of everything, leaving you bare,

you'll become one of many life lessons they'll share.
And you'll feel invisible, no longer there.

Analysing your thoughts sitting alone at night,
dark-tinted glasses will shade your sight.
Blaming yourself for all of the blight,
the darkness will come and dim your light.

Don't mask your pain with drugs or drink,
or into the dark hole you will sink.
My friend, be positive—that's all I ask.
Don't get caught up with the unchangeable
past.

Be strong and learn how to stand up tall.
Standing by your side, we won't allow you to fall.
I just need you to realise you're not alone.
In time, a new path will be shown.
Figure your route, plan the way,
and force the darkness to stay away.

Good times are coming. You will see.
This moment is a brief blip in history.
Focus on you and fixing your pain.
Realise you're not standing alone in the rain.
Please ask for help, for there is no shame.
There's more than one player allowed in this game.

Look in the mirror. Give that guy a break.
You only hate yourself because of the heartache.
Take this time for self-reflection,
make positive moves in life, and become the exception.

As I said before, please stand up tall.
I'm not willing to let you fall.
Together, soldier, we will sort a fix.
Trust me, brother, I've got your six.

Fear of the Unknown

It's your turn to shoot for the sky,
so make like a bird and begin to fly.
Why have you frozen? You look horrified.
It has been your dream; this you can't deny.

Are you worried that it's too high?
That you may fall and die?
Or is that fear I see in your eyes?
If you don't take your shot, life will pass you by.

If you don't take your go and let it drift on by,
you'll regret this moment till the day you die.
So seize your dreams. Take the opportunities as they arise.
If it doesn't work out, you can at least say you tried.

Adaptogen

These wrinkles that I wear upon my face
tell a story of my time in this place.
A life of broken promises, loss, and warfare
created the person you see standing here.
Not a thing I'd change, as a matter of fact.
This life has made me, so I'm happy with that.
It's had its ups and down, and sometimes I feel tested.
But mark my words, I'll never be bested!

Phoenix

Rise up, rise up,
like the new bird.
Rise up, rise up,
you're loved.

Bring light to your dark days.
Change your old ways.
From the ashes comes light;
from destruction comes life.
Give happiness something to measure;
replace the pain with pleasure.

Rise up, rise up,
like the new bird.
Rise up, rise up,
you're loved.

Dark clouds to blue skies,
clear those tears from your eyes.
Don't be the architect of your own demise.
Take knowledge from this moment;
use it to become wise.
Don't repeat the past. Your misery won't last.

Rise up, rise up,
like the new bird.
Rise up, rise up.
you're loved.

When you have no more to give,
feel there's no point to live,
when you've gone to every length,
from the fire draw strength.
When you hit the bottom
and feel forgotten . . .

remember:
rise up and feel love.
Rise up, you are loved.

Gratitude

I'm now grateful for life and all that it offers.
I'm grateful for my darling daughter.
I'm grateful for my health helping me live longer.
I'm grateful for the losses that have made me stronger.
I'm grateful for love from my friends and family.
I'm grateful for this newfound clarity.
I'm grateful for every single breath,
even the last at my death.

I'm grateful for all of these things and
excited to see what life will bring.

About the Author

William Farman McConville Currie is a British Army veteran. After spending several years in the Argyll and Sutherland Highlanders, gaining the rank of corporal, and seeing operational tours in Northern Ireland, Iraq, and Bosnia, he switched over to the private security sector and has provided close protection support to high-ranking military and government officials.

After an intense battle with depression, William felt as if a switch had been flipped in his brain, and he began to rhyme. He soon discovered that poetry helped release feelings previously stuck inside and decided to turn his new skill and passion toward writing a book that would shed light on the mental health and social issues veterans face. An ongoing mission, William continues to listen and offer his voice to his fellows in the struggle.

www.ingramcontent.com/pod-product-compliance
Lightning Source LLC
Chambersburg PA
CBHW050013040726
47599CB00014B/1357